HAZEL

C000131417

(THE MYSTERY OF HER DEATH)

BY

CHRISTINE BRIGHT

The twenty-year-old Hazel Drew lived a simple life before she turned 14 and began to work first as a domestic servant and later as a governess in the homes of wealthy men.

Hazel was discovered dead, floating in a Sand Lake Pool, causing dread in the hearts of many. This book looks at her controversial life as unmasked during investigations, the circumstances surrounding her death and the many and suspects.

Contents

CHAPTER ONE..4

INTRODUCTION 4

CHAPTER TWO..9

HAZEL'S DEATH 9

CHAPTER THREE......................................14

THE SHADY LIFE...............................14

CHAPTER FOUR.......................................21

SUSPECTS 21

CHAPTER ONE

INTRODUCTION

The twenty-year-old Hazel Drew was born on a farm, in East Poestenkill, New York, where she lived an ordinary farm life. At fourteen, she left to work in the home of a rich family, the family of the mayor of the city of Troy, later becoming a governess. Described as fair, blue-eyed and beautiful, the youthful woman worked hard and was liked by everyone. She was later employed by the family of a professor at her hometown of Sand Lake, where she had eventually settled at, working as a governess in his home. She is also known to have worked in the home of another powerful man in her town.

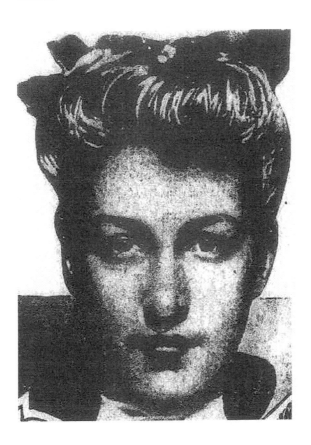

Hazel Drew via Times Union

In the evening of the 7th of July, 1908, Hazel Drew took a stroll along Taborton Road in Sand Lake. She was last seen four days before by Frank Smith, a teenager who worked at a farm closeby and Rudolph Gundrum, a charcoal seller who was about thirty-five. Around 7.30 pm, Frank had hailed Rudolph for a lift in his cart as she strolled, holding her hat in her hand and picking raspberries along the way. Her walk was easily noticed and remembered by the pair because of how uncommon it is to find a young woman of that age walking by herself.

Frank was in love with the young lady, a love which was not returned by her. Just like Frank, many other young men were trying to get to know her, with many of them mainly interested in courting and eventually marrying her, making her popular. This was primarily due to personality and beauty.

When Hazel was later seen, she was floating face down in the river. She was bloated and her skull had been crushed by an unidentified object. Her lungs were empty of water, meaning she was dead before she hit the lake and she was unrecognisable due to being in the water for four days.

She was identified easily by her gold filling and the cloth she wore, and as the inquiry into her death began, the details of her life started to come to light.

CHAPTER TWO

HAZEL'S DEATH

On July 7, 1908, twenty-year-old Hazel
Drew strolled up Taborton street
dressed as one going for a unique event.
It was Monday evening following the
July fourth end of the week.

Though it was boiling hot, Hazel wore
Victorian boots, white gloves, a dark
happy weather hat, and a triple-layered
dark skirt. She likewise wore her new
shirtwaist, one she had made quite
recently that Friday evening for an
eagerly awaited end of the week trip to
Lake George. An escape that was

strangely dropped the next Saturday morning.

Taborton street was only a little bigger than a heavily wooden cart trail cleared with rocks, similar as the mountain it ascended. Henry Rollman and his wife were advancing down Taborton to Averill Park when they saw a young lady picking berries by the roadside.

Mrs. Rollman remarked to her significant other,

"My isn't she pretty." Her husband concurred and added, "... yet she's a fool to be separated from everyone else on this street."

The Rollman's proceeded. It was getting dark at that moment, yet in the wake of driving an extensive distance, Mrs. Rollman turned back and saw Hazel was still standing all by herself in the Raspberry plot picking berries making Mrs. Rollman to say,

"My, yet that young lady is enjoying herself with those berries"

A post-mortem examination showed no hints of raspberries in Hazel's stomach.

Hazel was next seen by farmhand Frank Smith and charcoal merchant Rudy Gundrum at a turn in the street at what local people called "Piss Hollow."

Frank recognized and remembered Hazel as John Drew's girl, a young lady he knew and was affectionate of. Locals considered Frank as idiotic. This, alongside his activities that evening including, a 12 PM run into Averill Park, made him the most suspected of the crime.

Both Frank Smith and Rudy Gundrum dreaded the examination would end with their hanging.

This 7:30 pm locating of Hazel Irene Drew was the last time she was seen.

After four days, her body was found in similar garments face down in Teal

Pond, an area extremely near her last

locating.

CHAPTER THREE

THE SHADY LIFE

Only a few days before she was murdered, Hazel had resigned from her position at the mayor's home. Her reason remains unknown, but she was given the rest of her pay for the time she had worked and she left the house. She told her family that she had planned to travel but her exact travel plans was never revealed.

After Drew quit her place of employment, a friend saw her in the train station; Drew said that she was going "down the river," yet only one train was about leaving and it was bound north, for Albany. Drew was likewise definitely more social than her family at first revealed.

Hazel was also living well outside of her means. She was travelling first-class into New York city and to Rhode Island, dining at high class restaurants and staying in luxury hotels. Her new clothings were also far too costly for a woman who worked as house staff and e arned $3 a week.

According to her friends and family, there was no man in Hazel's life, but they probably knew a lot more than they were saying. Hazel's aunt refused to help the police and told a lot of Hazel's close friends to do the same.

Still, when questioned, Hazel's friend Carrie Weaver told investigators that Hazel had a way to make her money go further than a lot of people, and she had probably saved her earnings.

In May, just a few months before, Carrie and Hazel took a trip to New York where they spent time at the theatre, ate at high-end restaurants and stayed at a boarding house, despite Hazel losing her bag. Carrie said that they did not meet with any men while they were there, but Hazel had been to the city before then in the same month, on her own.

On the way home from New York, Hazel told her friend that she was going to spend the 4th of July holiday at Lake George, presumably with a man. When Independence Day weekend came, Hazel did not go to the lake, rather spening the holiday with her aunt.

However, Drew's auntie and family members initially depicted her to police and correspondents as a timid churchgoer and an indoor person "who was never out with young men,"

Investigators searched through Hazel's belongings and discovered a number of cards and letters from friends. There was also correspondence from a man known as C.E.S. The six letters he wrote were loving;

"Your (sic) happy smile and twinkling eyes torture me. Your face haunts me. Why can't I be contented again? You have stolen my liberty, please do not forget a pledge to write. When I reach Albany again, I'll meet you at the tavern. I must see you soon, or I will die of starvation."

Hazel's friends and family told investigators that they did not know who

C.E.S was and his identity was never discovered.

Also, on the 6th of July, Hazel was seen patiently waiting for a young, tall man at the train station. Those who saw them claimed the man had been really controlling over Hazel, but again, his identity was never discovered. Investigators had only a few leads to go on in the murder case that was beginning to capture the nation.

In one letter, a man named Harry apologized for causing a bruise on her wrists. He then, at that point, stated "I ought to live just for and have affectionate memories of my woman of the blond hair, and be steadfast onto death," which was "pretty scandalous for the time," it is said during a show at New York Comic Con on Oct. 8. Maybe, Drew in the long run had one more rough connection with "Henry" — or with another beau — that finished in her demise.

in addition to that, lots of handkerchief that were believed to belong to several men were found and it was believed that one of her proposals was from a man who was married at the time.

CHAPTER FOUR

SUSPECTS

Frank Smith was originally a suspect in the case because of his secret love for Hazel. The teenager was described as "dimwitted" and an easy suspect in the case. Still, Frank had an alibi and lots of witnesses for the night of the murder and was swiftly ruled out.

Another suspect in the death was Hazel's uncle William Taylor. He owned a farm nearby and although he was described as "odd", there was no substantiation that he had killed his niece and he was also released without charge.

Investigators had heard rumours about a dentist that Hazel was involved with, and according to The Evening Word, inquiries into thirty to forty dentists throughout Troy, New York began.

According to Hazel's friend, Mina Jones, the dentist had asked for Hazel's hand in marriage but his name was not known.

According to Mina, Hazel was also attacked about two times by a man a long time ago, and she managed to escape. He was however never caught.

While Drew's bosses were never accused of the crime nor blamed for it, two of them were hounded by outrages during the time that she worked for them, and she might have seen or heard something compromising that put her in harm's way.

Other people of interest included a man who lived in a mansion close by, organizing and seeking out orgies. He was originally suspected but on the night that Hazel died, shouts were coming from the home, inferring that the Albany millionaire was home.

Police spoke to Hazel's brother, Willie, who told them that he believed that when she took her last walk down Taborton Road, she was going to the ranch he was working at to say farewell to him. He said she would never leave without seeing him, and there was no other reason for her to be travelling down that specific road.

A grand jury ultimately assembled, the witnesses who had seen Hazel on the day of her murder and the days prior were brought in to give their accounts of what they had seen. There was no forensic evidence against any of the suspects, and the investigation went cold.

Could it be that one of her many secrets which her family and some friends worked hard to protect include the identity of her killer? Jarvis O'Brien, Rensselaer County district attorney in charge of the investigation, said that at a point in the investigation, he had a strong suspicion of who the murderer was but at the end of it, no body was officially accused, charged or sentenced for the crime.

Printed in Great Britain
by Amazon